She Persisted

NELLIE BLY

—INSPIRED BY—

She Persisted

by Chelsea Clinton & Alexandra Boiger

· ·

NELLIE BLY

· ·

Written by
Michelle Knudsen

Interior illustrations by
Gillian Flint

PHILOMEL

PHILOMEL BOOKS
An imprint of Penguin Random House LLC, New York

First published in the United States of America by Philomel,
an imprint of Penguin Random House LLC, 2021.

Visit us online at penguinrandomhouse.com.

Library of Congress Cataloging-in-Publication Data is available.

Printed in the United States of America

HC ISBN 9780593115749
PB ISBN 9780593115756

10 9 8 7 6 5 4 3 2 1

Edited by Jill Santopolo.
Design by Ellice M. Lee.
Text set in LTC Kennerley.

For
Ruby and Neve

She
Persisted

....

She Persisted: HARRIET TUBMAN

She Persisted: CLAUDETTE COLVIN

She Persisted: SALLY RIDE

She Persisted: VIRGINIA APGAR

She Persisted: NELLIE BLY

She Persisted: SONIA SOTOMAYOR

She Persisted: FLORENCE GRIFFITH JOYNER

She Persisted: RUBY BRIDGES

She Persisted: CLARA LEMLICH

She Persisted: MARGARET CHASE SMITH

She Persisted: MARIA TALLCHIEF

She Persisted: HELEN KELLER

She Persisted: OPRAH WINFREY

DEAR READER,

As Sally Ride and Marian Wright Edelman both powerfully said, "You can't be what you can't see." When Sally Ride said that, she meant that it was hard to dream of being an astronaut, like she was, or a doctor or an athlete or anything at all if you didn't see someone like you who already had lived that dream. She especially was talking about seeing women in jobs that historically were held by men.

I wrote the first *She Persisted* and the books that came after it because I wanted young girls—and children of all genders—to see women who worked hard to live their dreams. And I wanted all of us to see examples of persistence in the face of different challenges to help inspire us in our own lives.

I'm so thrilled now to partner with a sisterhood of writers to bring longer, more in-depth versions of these stories of women's persistence and achievement to readers. I hope you enjoy these chapter books as much as I do and find them inspiring and empowering.

And remember: If anyone ever tells you no, if anyone ever says your voice isn't important or your dreams are too big, remember these women. They persisted and so should you.

Warmly,

Chelsea Clinton

NELLIE BLY

TABLE OF CONTENTS

....

....

Pink

Nellie Bly spent her whole life doing things other people thought she couldn't. She spoke her mind in a time when women's voices often went unheard. She acted undercover to expose the truth about terrible injustices. And she performed amazing feats that made her one of America's most famous and daring reporters.

Nellie—though she didn't have that name yet—was born on May 5, 1864, in a small town not far from Pittsburgh, Pennsylvania. Her given name was Elizabeth Jane Cochran, but hardly anyone called her that. Thanks to her mother's habit of dressing her in pink and white (instead of the dull gray and brown most young girls wore), Elizabeth soon became known as "Pink."

Pink was a brown-haired girl who loved her family and chewing gum and horses. The town she was born in was called Cochran's Mills—it had once been Pitts' Mills, but the name was changed in honor of Pink's father, a successful property owner and mill operator who had been a local judge for five years. When Pink was five years old, her family moved to nearby Apollo, Pennsylvania. There she lived with her parents, three brothers, and one sister in a big house with enough land for a cow, a horse, and two dogs. She also had ten older

half siblings from her father's first marriage, which meant lots of half nieces, half nephews, and cousins to play with.

But soon something terrible happened—two months after Pink's sixth birthday, her beloved father unexpectedly died. He did not leave a will, and at that time husbands and wives did not automatically inherit each other's land and property. In order to divide his estate among his wife and many children, all of the property was sold at auction. Pink, her mother, and her young siblings lost their beautiful home and most of their money.

Pink's mother remarried two and a half years later. Her new husband, whose name was Jack, was nothing like Pink's father. Jack was often drunk and violent. More than once, he even threatened Pink's mother with a loaded gun! In those days it was very unusual for a woman to sue her husband for divorce, but Pink's mother finally decided she could not stay married to Jack. When Pink was fourteen years old, she, her brother Albert, and several neighbors testified in court about her stepfather's actions. Her mother was granted the divorce.

During this time, Pink learned that it wasn't always safe to rely on others for support. Her mother had thought each of her husbands would take care of her, but that had not turned out to be true. Pink became determined to take care of herself—and her mother as well. Training for a career seemed the best way to do that. At age fifteen, Pink decided to go to school to become a teacher.

The Indiana State Normal School was only fifteen miles away from Apollo and considered one of the best schools of its kind. "Normal schools" were places where young people could learn to be teachers or to work in business. When Pink enrolled, she added a silent "e" to the end of her last name. Perhaps she thought "Elizabeth J. Cochrane" sounded more fancy and sophisticated.

Pink was excited about school and wrote to her
brother Charles to tell him all about her fourth-
floor dorm room and her new roommate. She took
classes in arithmetic, grammar, reading, writing,
drawing, and spelling. She was looking forward to
becoming a teacher.

But near the end of her first year at school,
Pink discovered she would not be able to continue

her education. Pink had a little money held in her name at the bank. When she first decided to go to school, the banker in charge of managing that money had told her she would be able to afford the full three years required to become a teacher. But now he said she did not have enough money for even one more year. Pink could not believe it.

Upset and disappointed, she dropped out before taking her first-year final exams. Later in her life, embarrassed about her family's trouble with money, Pink would say that she had to drop out because she was ill, and also claimed she went to school for two years instead of just one. But money had been the real reason, and now she would have to find another way to earn a living. She was not going to let this setback stop her from taking care of her mother and herself.

The Girl Puzzle

The next year, Pink, her mother, and her two younger siblings moved to Allegheny City, where Pink's two older brothers had gone to find work. Pink tried to find work too, but there were few opportunities for young women. Pink's options were tutoring, nannying, or housekeeping, while her brothers, who had even less education than she did, were able to find higher-paying positions.

For four frustrating years, Pink worked odd

jobs. During that time, she often read a newspaper called the *Pittsburg Dispatch*, which by mid-1884 included the popular column Quiet Observations. Pink enjoyed reading the column until the author, a man named Erasmus Wilson, began writing about the role of women in society. Erasmus said that a woman's place was defined "by a single word—home" and, later, that a woman working outside the home was "a monstrosity." One day a man wrote to Erasmus about his five unmarried daughters and "what use to make of them." Erasmus responded in his column, complaining about the way girls were no longer raised into perfect future housewives who excelled at sewing, cooking, and cleaning.

Pink was furious when she read Erasmus's response. She wrote a letter to the *Dispatch* expressing her outrage, signing it "Lonely Orphan Girl."

Pink wasn't really an orphan, since her mother was still alive. But she probably signed her letter that way to remind readers who thought women should not work that not everyone had a working father or husband who could take care of them.

The letter caught the attention of George

Madden, the newspaper's managing editor. Although the letter wasn't very elegantly written, George admired the writer's spirit and her direct, serious tone. He showed it to Erasmus, saying, "She isn't much for style, but what she has to say she says it right out."

George placed a note in the paper asking the writer of the letter to come forward. The next day, a very nervous Pink climbed the four flights of stairs to the *Dispatch* newsroom and asked in a whisper where she could find the editor. When the office boy pointed to young, pleasant-faced George, Pink smiled. "Oh!" she exclaimed. "I expected to see an old, cross man." (*Cross* is a word that people used to use when they wanted to say someone was angry or grumpy.)

George asked Pink to write an article of her

own about the role of women. She went home and wrote "The Girl Puzzle." In her article, Pink argued that girls should be given the same chances as boys to start at the bottom of various professions and work their way up. She asked readers to think about women who had no choice but to work—poor women, or orphans, or those trying to support their families—and to have sympathy for them. It became her first published article, under the name "Orphan Girl." George paid her for it and immediately asked her to write another one.

He thought that Pink needed a better pen name if she was going to keep writing, though. At that time, it wasn't considered proper for a woman to write articles using her real name. Women wrote under made-up names instead, like Bessie

Bramble or Fanny Fern. George wanted Pink to have a name that was "neat and catchy." He asked his staff for ideas, and one of them suggested Nelly Bly, based on the song of that title by Stephen Collins Foster. George decided that name would do, but—possibly by mistake—he used a different spelling for Nellie.

Pink's new name appeared in the paper starting with her second article, which she wrote about divorce. She had strong feelings about that topic, remembering her mother's experience. Pink told George that for her next article, she wanted to write about the girls who worked in Pittsburgh factories. George offered her a position on the *Dispatch* staff, with a starting salary of five dollars a week.

Pink Elizabeth Jane Cochrane—now Nellie Bly—had finally found a job, but she had also found much more than that. She had found a way to speak out regarding the things she cared about. Perhaps, by writing of the world's injustices, she could convince other people to care about them too.

····························

CHAPTER 3

Newspaper Dreams

From the start, Nellie wrote in a way that grabbed readers' attention. She used vivid descriptions and unique details, and she wrote about people with compassion—she showed deep feeling for them and tried to understand their situations. After Nellie wrote eight articles about poor girls who worked in factories, George asked her to start writing so-called women's interest news— that meant things like fashion, gardening, and hair care. Nellie, however, hated writing those kinds of articles. She wanted to go to Mexico and write about what she saw there instead. George tried to talk her out of it. He thought it would be too dangerous. But Nellie didn't like when someone thought she couldn't do something. So she changed his mind.

Nellie brought her mother with her to Mexico

City. For five months Nellie sent the *Dispatch* her stories, which were published under the headline NELLIE IN MEXICO. She wrote about local people, local customs, bullfighting, and visiting American celebrities. She also wrote about the Mexican government's censorship of the press. This last topic eventually got her into trouble. She had to rush home one month earlier than planned when the government threatened to arrest her!

When she got back, George asked Nellie to focus on theater and culture writing. But after just a few months, Nellie had had enough. This wasn't the kind of reporting she wanted to do. One day she just stopped coming to work. "No one knew where she was," said Erasmus (also known as "Q.O.," for "Quiet Observer"), who had become Nellie's good friend. But then they found the note she had left:

DEAR Q.O.—I am off for New York.
Look out for me.

> *Bly.*

New York City was—as it remains today—the publishing capital of the country. Nellie arrived there in May 1887. She was twenty-one years old and certain that she would find a job at one of the city's big newspapers.

But no one would hire her.

In August, she had an idea. She decided to interview all the top newspaper editors for an article about whether New York was the best place for a woman to get started as a journalist. One after another, the editors told her why they didn't think women were as good as men at reporting. They said women weren't as accurate as men, that they often exaggerated, and that they couldn't be sent out on dangerous or late-night assignments. The ones who had hired women only wanted them to work on women's interest stories like the ones Nellie herself couldn't stand.

Her article about the interviews, which showed how prejudiced New York editors were against women, was published by the *Pittsburg Dispatch* and then picked up by other cities' newspapers. People all over the country were starting to notice Nellie, but it still didn't get her a job in New York. One day in September, she realized her purse was missing—and with it, the last of the little money she had left. She knew she had to do something fast. She was *not* going to return to Pittsburgh a failure.

Nellie borrowed ten cents for carfare from

her landlady and went straight to the downtown offices of the *World*—the most successful newspaper in the country and the one she most wanted to work for. When a clerk tried to send her away, Nellie insisted she had a very good idea for a story. If the editor wouldn't see her, then she would take her idea to some other paper.

Finally, she was allowed into Colonel John Cockerill's office. Nellie had met him while writing her article about women reporters and knew to

get straight to the point. She told him she wanted to travel from Europe to America on a ship, in steerage class, to write about what it was like for the many immigrants who traveled that way to the United States. After consulting with the owner of the newspaper, Cockerill offered Nellie a different idea instead. He asked if she would be willing to get herself locked in an insane asylum to report on what she found. Today, we have psychiatric hospitals where doctors help patients with mental illnesses. Back then, however, people who were mentally ill were often simply locked away in asylums or "madhouses." Many of those places were known for the horrible conditions inside.

"If you can do it," John Cockerill said, "it's more than anyone would believe."

·····························

CHAPTER 4

Going Undercover

The "madhouse" assignment was dangerous, but exciting—and it was something no woman had ever done before. Nellie was nervous but determined. She knew lots of people would think she couldn't do it. But she thought they were wrong.

Nellie fooled police officers, doctors, and nurses into believing she should be put in an asylum. She pretended to be confused and afraid,

said she didn't remember where she came from, and claimed to sometimes hear voices. Eventually she was taken to the asylum on New York City's Blackwell's Island (known today as Roosevelt Island)—a cold, frightening place where she found the patients being treated cruelly and given terrible food to eat. The nurses often punished them if they complained. Sometimes patients even died because of what the nurses did! Nellie also discovered that some of the women there were not actually mentally ill. Some were immigrants who simply could not speak English. Others had been sent there because of misunderstandings or mistakes. Some might even have been placed there just because other people wanted them out of the way. The doctors refused to listen when they tried to explain.

Once Nellie got to the asylum, she decided to act normally, other than continuing to hide her real name and purpose. But it made no difference: even though she was no longer pretending to be insane, the doctors and nurses still treated her as though she was.

After ten days, the newspaper sent people to bring Nellie home. Nellie wrote two long articles about the horrific conditions on Blackwell's Island, revealing the terrible truth and helping to bring about changes and better care for mental health patients. The editors let her sign her name to the first article, which was very rare. By the second article, her name was right in the headline. Newspapers all over North America picked up the story. Nellie's brave feat had made her famous. It also landed her a permanent job at the *World*.

Nellie had a special talent for undercover reporting. She took on different identities to write about everything from girls working in paper box factories to corrupt politicians to the illegal selling of babies whose parents could not take care of them. Today, most people don't approve of reporters pretending to be something they're not, but that wasn't the case in Nellie's time. The *World*'s editors wanted to get the truth for their readers however they could, and Nellie did too.

Nellie also had a unique way of writing her stories from her own point of view, including her opinions and feelings about her topics. Many journalists today try to be more objective, but Nellie's readers loved hearing her personal thoughts in her articles. In addition to her undercover work, she often tried out different professions and experiences to write about, like performing onstage as a chorus girl and learning how to fence.

Nellie was making enough money by now to bring her mother to New York to live with her. In just her first year as a New York reporter, she had achieved more success than anyone ever expected.

In the fall of 1888, Nellie interviewed Belva

Lockwood—the first woman to practice law before the Supreme Court. Ms. Lockwood was running for president for the second time, thirty-two years before American women had won the right to vote. Nellie wrote about whether women should propose marriage to men, almost got her healthy tonsils operated on during another undercover stunt, and was called an "audacious investigator of abuses" in a magazine article about women reporters of the time. *Audacious* means fearless and daring, and it was a good word to describe Nellie. She interviewed other courageous women too, including a young deaf and blind girl named Helen Keller.

But the achievement that made Nellie the most famous was still to come.

Nellie's work for the *World* had made the newspaper even more popular. Its circulation—the number of copies it sold—was higher than any other newspaper, but when the numbers started to go down slightly, the editors wanted something big to capture the public's interest. Nellie had proposed just such an idea a year earlier, but the newspaper editors had said no. Now they decided the time had come to try it.

What was the idea? Nellie would attempt to travel around the entire world faster than anyone ever had before.

CHAPTER 5

....

Around the World

When Nellie first suggested her around-the-world idea, the newspaper manager said that only a man could do such a thing. He claimed a woman wouldn't be able to travel alone, and that she would need to bring too much luggage.

"Very well," Nellie said angrily. "Start the man and I'll start the same day for some other newspaper and beat him."

John Cockerill thought Nellie might do just

that. He promised her that if they ever decided to send a reporter on this assignment, she would be the one to go.

A year later, Nellie's editor called her into the office on a cold and rainy evening. "Can you start around the world day after tomorrow?"

"I can start this minute," Nellie said at once, her heart pounding with excitement.

Her ship wasn't leaving that minute, though, so she had one full day to get ready. To prove the newspaper manager wrong, and to make sure her luggage wouldn't slow her down, Nellie packed only one small bag to bring on her trip. In addition to her writing tools and other supplies, she brought several changes of underwear but just one dress. She would wear that one dress for her entire journey.

Nellie wanted to beat the imaginary record

set in Jules Verne's famous novel *Around the World in Eighty Days*. No one in real life had ever traveled around the world that fast. Nellie thought she could do it in only seventy-five days.

Today, someone could circle the world much faster. But in the 1800s, passenger planes hadn't been invented yet. Nellie would have to travel by steamship, train, and ferry.

On November 14, 1889, at exactly 9:40 a.m. and thirty seconds, Nellie waved good-bye from the deck of a ship called the *Augusta Victoria* as it sailed away from Hoboken Pier.

"Do you get seasick?" someone asked her.

Almost immediately, to her great embarrassment, she did. But eventually Nellie got used to being at sea, and she was able to start to enjoy herself.

There was something Nellie didn't know,

however. When the owner of New York's *Cosmopolitan Magazine* heard about Nellie's trip, he decided to send his own reporter to race against her! Twenty-eight-year-old Elizabeth Bisland left New York just a few hours after Nellie, heading west by train while Nellie headed east by ship. For the next two and a half months, the world would watch breathlessly as these two young women raced each other all the way around the earth.

When Nellie got to London, she learned that Jules Verne and his wife had invited her to visit their home in France. Nellie couldn't pass up the chance to meet them, even though it meant she had to skip two nights' sleep in order to stay on schedule. Jules Verne was excited about her journey, and he marked her route on a map beside the route his character Phileas Fogg had taken in the book. "Godspeed," the Vernes wished her as she left. "Good luck."

From France she traveled to Italy, then Egypt, then through the places that are now called Yemen, Sri Lanka, and Malaysia to Singapore. While in

Singapore, Nellie bought a pet monkey that she named McGinty. McGinty was Nellie's traveling companion for the rest of the trip (and went home to live with her afterward!).

Her next stop was Hong Kong, and it was there that Nellie found out about Elizabeth Bisland. A man in the steamship office told her, "You are going to be beaten." He explained that Elizabeth had already been there before her and traveled on for Singapore. Nellie was shocked and confused. Hiding her feelings, she told the man that she had promised her editor to go around the world in seventy-five days, and if she succeeded in that, she would be satisfied.

"I am not racing with anyone," she said. "If someone else wants to do the trip in less time, that is their concern."

Back home, people kept buying the newspaper to read about Nellie's adventures. The *World* sold even more papers when they decided to run a contest. Whoever guessed closest to the exact time of Nellie's journey would win their own first-class trip to Europe.

Nellie continued on to Japan, then sailed to San Francisco and raced by train back across the United States. In the end, she did beat Elizabeth Bisland, and even beat her own original goal. Instead of seventy-five days, Nellie made it around the world in seventy-two days, six hours, eleven minutes, and fourteen seconds.

CHAPTER 6

....

More Surprises

That trip made Nellie the most talked-about woman in America. Women around the country began wearing Nellie Bly caps, dresses, and gloves modeled on the ones she wore on her trip. There was even a Nellie Bly board game! But although Nellie's amazing journey had made lots of money for the *World* newspaper, the editors never properly thanked her or gave her any kind of raise or reward. Nellie was so hurt and angry that she quit.

She didn't think she would ever go back, but when a new editor took over the Sunday edition of the *World* three years later, he immediately offered her a job. She agreed to write for the *World* again, and her first article appeared right on the front page. She went on to write about many things, including a series about the Pullman railroad strike in Chicago that would be remembered as some of her best reporting.

Nellie wasn't finished surprising the world, however. In 1895, she suddenly got married to a seventy-year-old millionaire she had met only two weeks before. She started working in her husband's company—the Iron Clad Manufacturing Company—and eventually became its president. When her husband died, she took over the business. She cared deeply about her employees and took

good care of them. She gave them weekly wages (instead of only paying them for each individual piece of work), built a multi-floor recreation center for them to use, and even kept a mini hospital on Iron Clad property. She was one of the few women in the world managing such a large company, and for a while it was very successful. But dishonest managers stole money from the business, and eventually the company went bankrupt.

In 1914, Nellie decided to visit a friend in Vienna, Austria. Four days before she was supposed to leave, World War I began in Europe. Nellie boarded her ship anyway and ended up reporting on the war from the eastern front.

Nellie stayed in Europe for four and a half years, reporting on the horrors she witnessed and promoting war relief efforts. Once back home, she continued to write articles, this time taking a job with the *New York Evening Journal*. She also began to write an advice column, and she tried especially to help women in need of work and children in need of homes. She received so many letters that by October 1919, people had to wait eight weeks for a response. But Nellie tried to help as many of them as she could.

Nellie kept writing and trying to help people for as long as she lived. She worked so hard, in fact, that her health suffered. She died at only fifty-seven years of age.

Nellie's determination had transformed not only her own life, but the lives of so many others as well. "Energy rightly applied and directed," Nellie once said, "will accomplish anything."

And that is a gift that Nellie gave to the women of her time and all the women who came after her: she proved that with persistence and perseverance, women everywhere could achieve great things—no matter who tried to tell them they couldn't. So can you.

HOW YOU CAN PERSIST

by Michelle Knudsen

If you would like to help carry on Nellie Bly's legacy, there are a lot of things you can do. Here are some ideas:

1. Join your school's newspaper or magazine club—or start one if your school doesn't have one yet!

2. Keep a journal and write down your thoughts, feelings, and ideas.

3. Write letters asking your elected representatives to fight for equal pay for women and minorities (women and minorities are still often paid less money for the same work).

4. Start a scrapbook of places around the world you might want to travel to someday.

5. Read books and articles written by women, and watch movies and shows created and directed by women.

6. Try something new—an activity, a sport, even a kind of food—that you've never tried before.

7. Encourage your friends to pursue their own dreams and support them as much as you can.

8. Tell your friends and family the story of Nellie Bly. Tell them how she persisted even though her father died, even though her family didn't have enough money to keep her in school, and even though many people thought women could never be as good at reporting as men. Tell them how Nellie proved those people wrong.

ACKNOWLEDGMENTS

....

I owe a great debt to others who have written about the life of Nellie Bly, especially Brooke Kroeger, whose excellent biography and extensive notes were an invaluable resource while writing this book. Thanks also to my agent, Jodi Reamer (as always), for her unwavering support and encouragement, to my editors, Talia Benamy and Jill Santopolo, for helping me make this book the best it could be, and to Chelsea Clinton and Philomel Books for creating this wonderful series in the first place and allowing me to be a part of it. Nellie Bly is an inspiration, and I hope more readers continue to discover her amazing story and carry on her legacy of audacious perseverance.

Most of all, thank you to my very understanding family who let me hide away so often to research and write (and to our cats, who kept me company during late-night working sessions after everyone else had gone to sleep).

◦ References ◦

Bernard, Diane. "She Went Undercover
to Expose an Insane Asylum's Horrors.
Now Nellie Bly Is Getting Her Due." *The
Washington Post*, July 28, 2019. https://www
.washingtonpost.com/history/2019/07/28
/she-went-undercover-expose-an-insane-asylums
-horrors-now-nellie-bly-is-getting-her-due.

Bly, Nellie. "Among the Mad." *Godey's Lady's Book* 118, no. 703 (January 1, 1889): 20, 83. http://sites.dlib.nyu.edu/undercover/sites/dlib .nyu.edu.undercover/files/documents/uploads /editors/Among-The-Mad-NellieBly1889.pdf.

———. *Around the World in Seventy-Two Days and Other Writings*. Edited by Jean Marie Lutes. New York: Penguin Classics, 2014.

———. "Mad Marriages." *Pittsburg Dispatch*, February 1, 1885. https://efbbc0aa -141e-46c5-b161-0aa2d1550ca8.filesusr.com/ugd /d9c14a_5fe8bff57798482d98a4dfd292a7fe0a .pdf.

———. *Six Months in Mexico*. New York: American Publishers Corporation, 1888.

———. *Ten Days in a Madhouse*. 1887. Read by Laural Merlington. Tantor Audiobook Classics. Old Saybrook, Connecticut: 2011. Sound file.

———. "Trying to Be a Servant." *New York World*, October 30, 1887. http://sites.dlib.nyu .edu/undercover/sites/dlib.nyu.edu.undercover /files/documents/uploads/editors/Trying-to-be-a -servant.pdf.

———. "Visiting the Dispensaries." *New York World*, December 2, 1888. https:// undercover.hosting.nyu.edu/files/original /fde0c99403e55957055eacab87772c79d2b14d96.pdf.

———. "What Becomes of Babies?" *New York World*, November 6, 1887. http://sites.dlib.nyu .edu/undercover/sites/dlib.nyu.edu .undercover/files/documents/uploads/editors /What-Becomes-of-Babies.pdf.

———. "Women Journalists." *Pittsburg Dispatch*, August 21, 1887. https://efbbc0aa -141e-46c5-b161-0aa2d1550ca8.filesusr.com/ugd /d9c14a_154f30c4e99541b0b0002565ad0b7797 .pdf; https://efbbc0aa-141e-46c5-b161 -0aa2d1550ca8.filesusr.com/ugd /d9c14a_86356554ebdf420c939ca82f11f9d553.pdf.

———. "Working Girls Beware!" *New York World*, February 3, 1889. http://sites.dlib.nyu .edu/undercover/sites/dlib.nyu.edu

.undercover/files/documents/uploads/editors
/Working-Girls-Beware.pdf.

Boardman, Samantha, M.D., and George J.
Makari M.D. "The Lunatic Asylum on
Blackwell's Island and the New York Press."
American Journal of Psychiatry 164, no. 4
(April 2007): 581. https://ajp.psychiatryonline
.org/doi/pdfplus/10.1176/ajp.2007.164.4.581.

Fessenden, Marissa. "Nellie Bly's Record-
Breaking Trip Around the World Was,
to Her Surprise, A Race." *Smithsonian
Magazine*, January 25, 2016. https://
www.smithsonianmag.com/smart-news
/nellie-blys-record-breaking-trip-around-world
-was-to-her-surprise-race-180957910.

Goodman, Matthew. *Eighty Days: Nellie Bly and Elizabeth Bisland's History-Making Race Around the World*. New York: Ballantine Books, 2013.

Horn, Stacy. *Damnation Island: Poor, Sick, Mad & Criminal in 19th-Century New York*. New York: Algonquin Books of Chapel Hill, 2018.

Kroeger, Brooke. *Nellie Bly: Daredevil, Reporter, Feminist*. New York: Random House, 1994.

Lane, Penny, dir. *Undercover in an Insane Asylum: How a 23-Year-Old Changed Journalism*. Center for Investigative Reporting/Glassbreaker Films. 2017. https://www.theatlantic.com/video/index/590464/nellie-bly.

Markel, Howard. "How Nellie Bly Went
    Undercover to Expose Abuse of the Mentally
    Ill." Nation. *PBS NewsHour.* May 5, 2018.
    https://www.pbs.org/newshour/nation
    /how-nellie-bly-went-undercover-to-expose
    -abuse-of-the-mentally-ill.

Noyes, Deborah. *Ten Days a Madwoman:*
    The Daring Life and Turbulent Times of the
    Original "Girl" Reporter Nellie Bly. New York:
    Viking, 2016.

Phelan, Matt. *Around the World.* Somerville:
    Candlewick Press, 2011.

"What Was Blackwell's Island?" New-York
    Historical Society Museum & Library and

NYC Media, 2011. https://www.nyhistory .org/community/blackwells-island.

Wilson, Erasmus. *Quiet Observations on the Ways of the World*. New York: Cassell, 1886.

MICHELLE KNUDSEN is the *New York Times* bestselling author of fifty books for young readers of all ages, including the award-winning picture book *Library Lion*, which was selected by *Time* magazine as one of the 100 Best Children's Books of All Time. Her other books include the picture book *Marilyn's Monster* (one of NPR's Best Books of 2015) and the novels *The Dragon of Trelian* (VOYA Top Shelf Fiction for Middle School Readers) and *Evil Librarian* (YALSA Best Fiction for Young Adults and winner of the Sid Fleischman Award for Humor). Michelle also works as a freelance editor and writing teacher and serves on the Writing for Young People MFA faculty at Lesley University. She lives in Brooklyn, New York.

You can visit Michelle Knudsen online at
micheleknudsen.com
or follow her on Twitter
@michelleknudsen
and on Instagram
@michelle.knudsen

GILLIAN FLINT has worked as a professional illustrator since earning an animation and illustration degree in 2003. Her work has since been published in the UK, USA and Australia. In her spare time, Gillian enjoys reading, spending time with her family and puttering about in the garden on sunny days. She lives in the northwest of England.

You can visit Gillian Flint online at
gillianflint.com
or follow her on Twitter
@GillianFlint
and on Instagram
@gillianflint_illustration

CHELSEA CLINTON is the author of the #1 *New York Times* bestseller *She Persisted: 13 American Women Who Changed the World*; *She Persisted Around the World: 13 Women Who Changed History*; *She Persisted in Sports: American Olympians Who Changed the Game*; *Don't Let Them Disappear: 12 Endangered Species Across the Globe*; *It's Your World: Get Informed, Get Inspired & Get Going!*; *Start Now!: You Can Make a Difference*; with Hillary Clinton, *Grandma's Gardens* and *Gutsy Women*; and, with Devi Sridhar, *Governing Global Health: Who Runs the World and Why?* She is also the Vice Chair of the Clinton Foundation, where she works on many initiatives, including those that help empower the next generation of leaders. She lives in New York City with her husband, Marc, their children and their dog, Soren.

Courtesy of the author

You can follow Chelsea Clinton on Twitter
@ChelseaClinton
or on Facebook at
facebook.com/chelseaclinton

ALEXANDRA BOIGER has illustrated nearly twenty picture books, including the She Persisted books by Chelsea Clinton; the popular Tallulah series by Marilyn Singer; and the Max and Marla books, which she also wrote. Originally from Munich, Germany, she now lives outside of San Francisco, California, with her husband, Andrea, daughter, Vanessa, and two cats, Luiso and Winter.

You can visit Alexandra Boiger online at
alexandraboiger.com
on follow her on Instagram
@alexandra_boiger

Don't miss the rest of the books in the

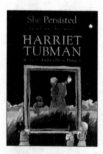

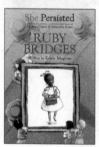

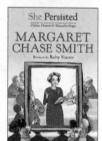

She Persisted series!

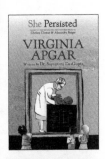

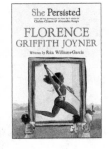

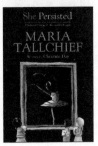